21st Century Skills Library

COOL CAREERS

SPORTS MEDICINE DOCTOR

Patricia K. Kummer

Cherry Lake Publishing
Ann Arbor, Michigan

CHERRY LAKE
Publishing

Published in the United States of America by Cherry Lake Publishing
Ann Arbor, Michigan
www.cherrylakepublishing.com

Content Adviser: Thomas Sawyer EdD, Professor of Recreation and Sports Management, Indiana State University

Photo Credits: Cover and pages 1, 11, and 16 ©JUPITERIMAGES/Comstock Images/ Alamy; page 4, ©JUPITERIMAGES/Thinkstock/Alamy; page 6, ©Mary Evans Picture Library/Alamy; page 8, ©Wendy Nero, used under license from Shutterstock, Inc.; page 12, ©dasilva, used under license from Shutterstock, Inc.; page 14, ©Laurence Gough, used under license from Shutterstock, Inc.; page 19, ©Corbis Super RF/Alamy; page 20, ©Kiselev Andrey Valerevich, used under license from Shutterstock, Inc.; page 22, ©Peter Carroll/Alamy; page 25, ©Corbis Premium RF/Alamy; page 27, ©Corbis RF/Alamy

Library of Congress Cataloging-in-Publication Data
Kummer, Patricia K.
Sports medicine doctor / Patricia K. Kummer.
    p. cm.—(Cool careers)
Includes index.
ISBN-13: 978-1-60279-302-6
ISBN-10: 1-60279-302-6
1. Sports medicine—Vocational guidance—Juvenile literature.
2. Sports physicians—Juvenile literature. I. Title. II. Series.
RC1210.K86 2009
617.1'027023—dc22   2008011626

Cherry Lake Publishing would like to acknowledge the work of
The Partnership for 21st Century Skills.
Please visit www.21stcenturyskills.org for more information.

TABLE OF CONTENTS

CHAPTER ONE

FROM ANCIENT TIMES TO TODAY

X-rays are an important tool for sports medicine doctors. They help doctors spot broken bones.

The star forward is fouled and knocked to the floor. He grabs his shoulder in great pain. The college team's sports medicine doctor runs onto the court. The doctor can tell by looking at it that the shoulder joint has been badly hurt. The player is helped off the court and taken to the hospital. The player has several tests and X-rays done on his shoulder. In a few days, an **orthopedic surgeon** will perform **arthroscopic surgery**. After a long period of **rehabilitation**, the player will rejoin the team next season.

Examining, identifying, and treating sports injuries are some of the things sports doctors do. They have a special interest in treating injuries to muscles, bones, and joints. For most sports doctors, working with a team is only one part of their **medical practice**. They also treat anyone who is physically active. Their patients may include people who are dancers or who enjoy running, golfing, or other sports activities. For sports doctors, an **athlete** is anyone who is physically active or involved in sports.

Doctors have been treating athletes' injuries for more than 2,000 years. Many historians trace the beginning of sports medicine to the Greeks. Hippocrates (460–375 BCE), an ancient Greek doctor, is known as the Father of

Some of Galen's work involved studying the spinal cord and muscles.

Medicine. Galen (139–199 CE), another Greek doctor,
is best known for his work with Roman gladiators and
chariot drivers. He also served as the doctor of three
Roman emperors. These early doctors used some of the
same types of supplies to treat athletes as are used by

sports doctors today. **Splints** kept injured joints from moving. Casts helped broken bones to heal. Stitches closed wounds. Galen even made a medicine to ease muscle **sprains** and **strains**.

About 1,000 years later, scientists and doctors were still learning about the human body. Leonardo da Vinci (1452–1519), the Italian artist and scientist, studied and made sketches of how people moved. He also wrote reports about how the body changes during exercise. In 1569, the Italian doctor Geronimo Mercuriali (1530–1606) wrote the first illustrated book on sports medicine. It had pictures of people climbing ropes and using medicine balls for exercise. These studies led to the advancement of modern sports medicine doctors.

During the 1800s, some U.S. colleges started programs in gymnastics and football. These colleges hired doctors to care for their athletes' injuries. In 1896, the Olympic

Today, sports medicine doctors treat people of all ages who play all kinds of sports.

Games were restarted. Doctors later became part of the Games. They made sure that athletes passed physical examinations before competing.

In 1928, doctors from several countries met in Switzerland and founded the International Assembly on Sports Medicine. Since the 1930s, sports doctors have established basic rules of sports medicine. For example, athletes should have a physical examination before the start of each season. Another rule is that only a doctor—not a coach— should decide if an athlete is ready to return to the sport after an injury.

Today, more and more people of all ages are taking part in sports and are exercising. When

21st Century Content

In 1937, Ruth Jackson became the first female orthopedic surgeon in the United States. Every year, more and more females become involved in team sports and individual exercise activities. However, less than 11 percent of people preparing to be orthopedic surgeons are female.

In recent years, studies have found that knee injuries differ between men and women. This is important because most male sports doctors use the same type of treatments on women as they do on men. Women and girls need different treatments than men and boys.

What do you think should be done to attract more women into the career of sports doctor? Do you think more female sports doctors would improve the care of female athletes? Why or why not?

they are injured, a sports doctor treats many of them. These doctors use the same equipment and treatments on them as are used on college and professional athletes. Improvements have been made in preventing and treating sports injuries. Every year, better, safer, and stronger sports equipment is designed. Sports doctors have played an important role in encouraging the development of these designs.

CHAPTER TWO

WHAT IT TAKES TO BE A SPORTS DOCTOR

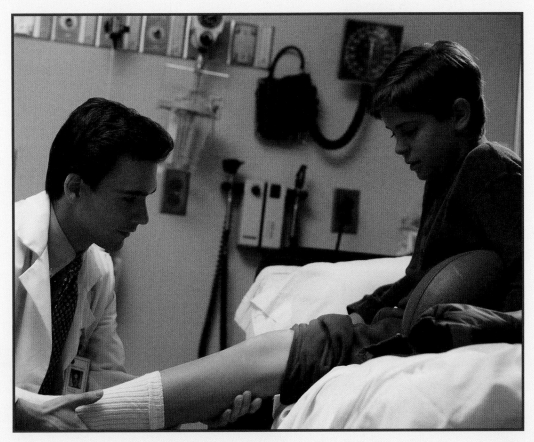

Sports doctors do not just treat injuries that occur from sports accidents. They also treat injuries that develop gradually over time.

Becoming a sports doctor takes several years of education and training. Training is long and difficult because the career of sports doctor is highly specialized. All doctors

Sports doctors must have good communication skills.

choose an area of medicine to specialize in. Many of them choose family practice, pediatrics, orthopedics, or emergency medicine. Some of these specialists then become even more specialized. They become sports doctors.

Sports doctors must have good "people skills" because they must work with many kinds of people. They have to get their ideas across to the athletes they treat. They must also talk to the athlete's parents or other family members. If the athlete is on a team, the sports doctor must communicate with the athlete's coach. Sports doctors have to be able to communicate easily with others.

Sports doctors should enjoy working with people who like to be physically active. It helps if sports doctors have experience playing sports or taking part in physical activities. Having had a sports injury of some kind can be helpful. Then the sports doctor better understands what his or her patients are going through.

An interest in becoming a sports medicine doctor can begin at an early age. In elementary school, students can start learning about this career. Articles in sports

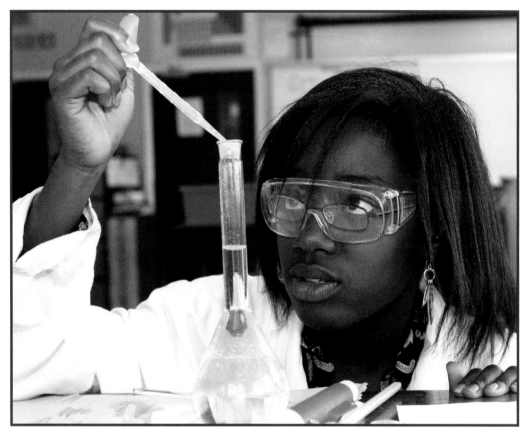

*Taking extra science classes is a smart step
toward a sports medicine career.*

magazines, in sports sections of newspapers, and on
the Internet are good sources of information. Students
can also interview sports medicine doctors. Teachers or
parents can set up a tour for students at a sports
medicine clinic.

Students can also prepare for this career in high school. They should take as many science classes as possible. Classes should include biology, chemistry, and psychology. Students preparing to be sports doctors must have good grades in these and other classes. They should also participate in sports. In addition, they could work as an assistant to the school's sports doctor or athletic trainer.

Students must go to college to become sports medicine doctors. Many enroll in a premedical program. In this program, they take many science classes. These classes include anatomy, biology, chemistry, **physiology**, and mathematics. During the third year of college, anyone planning on being a doctor must take the MCAT. This is the Medical College Admission Test. Students must receive a high score on this test. Only students with high college grades and high MCAT scores are admitted to medical school.

Medical school students must study very hard. Professors want to make sure that only students who are serious about becoming doctors graduate.

There are more than 120 medical schools in the United States. Medical school is a four-year program. During the first two years, students spend most of their time in the classroom. They take more science classes. These classes include anatomy, biochemistry, microbiology, physiology, and the study of prescription drugs. They also study legal and ethical issues of medical practice. During the last two years of medical school, medical students gain real experience. They learn how to work with patients. They spend many hours in hospitals and are guided by doctors. At the end of the four years, medical students receive the doctor of medicine degree (MD). Now they can be called "doctor," but they cannot practice as a doctor. They still have several more years of training to complete.

After medical school, some doctors spend a year working in a hospital. This is sometimes called an internship. During the internship, new doctors gain more experience. After completing the internship, they take a licensing examination in their state. When they pass this test, they are licensed to practice medicine.

But most doctors complete their intern year as part of a multiyear residency program. As residents, doctors learn

a medical specialty such as pediatrics or orthopedics. When they finish the residency program, they take tests in their specialty. After passing these tests, they become **certified** to practice their medical specialty.

The final step in becoming a sports doctor is enrolling in a sports medicine fellowship program. These specialized training programs train doctors to prevent, identify, and treat sports injuries. Doctors spend one or two years in the sports medicine fellowship. In the United States, there are more than 120 sports medicine fellowship programs.

CHAPTER THREE

THE WORK OF SPORTS DOCTORS

*A sports doctor takes the height and weight of
a patient during a physical exam.*

The main work of sports doctors is to prevent and
to treat injuries in athletes. To prevent injuries, sports
doctors usually perform a physical examination before an

A doctor may advise an athlete to eat more fresh fruits and vegetables.

athlete takes part in a sport. The exam might show that an athlete is overweight or underweight. It might show that an athlete should build up strength in a muscle. It might also show that a joint does not move as far or as easily as it should. The sports doctor then suggests exercises or a change in diet. After this exam, the sports doctor will see these athletes in follow-up visits to make sure that their health is improving.

Sports doctors must also identify and treat injuries to athletes. Most of these injuries involve broken bones, strained muscles, sprained ligaments, and damaged joints. First, the doctor determines the amount of damage. This can sometimes be done by looking at or feeling the injury. Sometimes an ice pack or heat pack is all that is needed. Sometimes a sports doctor orders an X-ray of the painful joint to see how badly it is injured.

Arthrography is another way of determining joint injuries. The doctor injects dye into the injured joint. Then another X-ray is taken. It shows more clearly where the injury is and how bad it is. In more serious injuries, sports doctors use an arthroscope to see the damage. They might also use the arthroscope to perform surgery. Sports doctors who are also orthopedic surgeons perform this type

Ankle injuries are one common problem treated by sports medicine doctors.

of surgery. Sometimes an athlete's knee, hip, or shoulder joint is greatly damaged and must be replaced. Then the sports doctor performs an **arthroplasty**. In this operation, the damaged joint is replaced with one made of metal or plastic.

Sports doctors may also prescribe rehabilitation programs to athletes. Rehabilitation programs start after an injury has healed. Exercise is usually a large part of most rehabilitation programs. These programs help athletes rebuild strength. They also help athletes regain flexibility.

Most sports doctors work in a sports medicine clinic or hospital. They may work with several other sports doctors. These doctors share equipment and other staff, such as nurses and record keepers. Sports doctors see most of their patients in the clinic. This is where they perform physical examinations. This is also where they check patients' progress with rehabilitation exercises.

Many sports doctors also work with athletes on high school or

When an athlete is injured, the sports doctor is not the only one concerned with the athlete's well-being. In most cases, a whole team of people is involved. The athlete and the athlete's parents or other family members are part of this team. Sometimes a coach is involved. The sports doctor may bring in other people with special skills to the team. These specialists might include a physical therapist, an occupational therapist, a nutritionist or dietician, or an athletic trainer. To learn more about these occupations, go to www.bls.gov/oco/home.htm.

college teams. These doctors give team members physical examinations. Sports doctors who work with a team usually attend all games both at home and away. Sometimes athletes are injured during a game. The sports doctor decides if the injured player should be taken out of the game. The sports doctor also makes the final decision about an athlete returning to the team after an injury.

A few sports doctors work with professional sports teams. Some work with individual professional athletes such as figure skaters or golfers. It takes many years of experience before sports doctors are hired to work with professional athletes. These doctors are some of the best-known people in their field. Many of these sports doctors are also orthopedic surgeons. They are called in to repair the damage that sports injuries have caused. Surgeries take place in hospital operating rooms.

CHAPTER FOUR

A Look Ahead for Sports Doctors

Sports doctors sometimes have patients use special exercise bands. These bands stretch to help a person build strength.

Each year more people take part in sports. Some join their company's softball team. Others start running or using weights. Many people are staying physically active

later in life. Some 80-year-olds are still playing golf. Sports injuries can happen to any of these people. Sports doctors are there to help all of them.

Sports doctors should expect many changes in their career. The number of jobs for them will continue to increase because so many people are becoming physically active. More people will need sports doctors to help them avoid injury and treat any injuries that do happen.

Sports teams at all levels are expected to hire more sports doctors. Some experts believe that owners of professional athletic teams will add more specialists to their staffs. These sports doctors will specialize in injuries to certain parts of the body. More

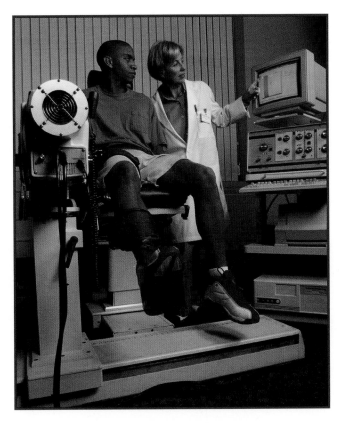

Doctors may use special sensors to study the way an athlete moves. This information can help prevent injury.

high schools will start to hire sports doctors, at least on a part-time basis.

Doctors and scientists continue to develop new tools and equipment for treating injuries. They also develop more effective exercises for rehabilitation. Much of the new equipment for surgery and rehabilitation uses computers. Some of the new ways of doing surgery require doctors to use remote-controlled instruments. All of these improvements help people return to their sport or activity faster after an injury. To help their patients, sports doctors will have to keep up with these changes. They will have to become experts at using these new treatments, tools, and equipment.

Being a sports doctor has many good points. Sports doctors earn a lot of money. If they practice in clinics, their average salary could be $200,000. Those who are also orthopedic surgeons could earn more than $375,000 a year. Sports doctors who work for professional sports teams have the highest earnings. They can earn $1 million or more a year.

Do you like to help people get and stay physically active? Do you like working with people in a variety of different situations? If you answered yes to these questions, and if you get good grades in school—especially in science— then being a sports medicine doctor may be a good career choice for you.

Some Famous Sports Doctors

James R. Andrews (1942–) is one of the pioneers of arthroscopic surgery and is best-known for advancing the field of elbow, knee, and shoulder surgery. In 1986, Dr. Andrews co-founded the Alabama Sports Medicine and Orthopedic Center in Birmingham. Later, he co-founded the American Sports Medicine Institute.

Jack C. Hughston (1917–2004) was an orthopedic surgeon and is known as one of the fathers of sports medicine. In 1949, he founded the Hughston Clinic in Columbus, Georgia. When the Hughston Sports Medicine Hospital opened in 1984, it was the only sports medicine hospital in the country. In 1972, he founded the American Journal of Sports Medicine.

David H. Janda (1958–) founded the Institute for Preventive Sports Medicine (IPSM) in Ann Arbor, Michigan, in 1989, shortly after becoming an orthopedic surgeon. The IPSM does research to find ways to make sports and sports equipment safer for athletes.

Lyle J. Micheli (1940?–) is an orthopedic surgeon and the director of the Division of Sports Medicine at Children's Hospital in Boston. He is also the doctor for the Boston Ballet and the Boston Ballet School. Dr. Micheli has written two popular books, The Sports Medicine Bible (1995) and The Sports Medicine Bible for Young Athletes (2001).

Jacquelin Perry (1928–), an orthopedic surgeon, is considered one of the pioneers in sports medicine. She is known throughout the world for her gait studies—studying how the foot moves during walking. Her textbook on gait is still considered the best book on that subject.

Dr. Augustus Thorndike (1896–1986) is known as one of the fathers of sports medicine. He worked with the athletic department at Harvard University from 1931 to 1962. In 1938, he published Athletic Injuries, Prevention, Diagnosis, and Treatment, the first U.S. book on sports medicine.

GLOSSARY

arthrography (ar-THRUH-graf-ee) a way of determining joint injuries by injecting dye into an injured joint and then taking an X-ray

arthroplasty (AR-thruh-plass-tee) an operation in which damaged joints are replaced with new joints made of plastic or metal

arthroscopic surgery (ar-thruh-SCAH-pik SUR-juh-ree) an operation in which a doctor makes a small cut, inserts a narrow tube equipped with a camera to view a joint, and then repairs any damage to the joint

athlete (ATH-leet) a person who is skilled at playing a sport or sports

certified (SUR-tuh-fyed) officially approved to be able to do a job, usually after passing a test

ligaments (LIG-uh-muhntz) thick bands of tissue that connect one bone to another bone

medical practice (MED-uh-kuhl PRAK-tiss) the business or work of a doctor

orthopedic surgeon (or-thuh-PEE-dik SUR-juhn) a doctor who performs operations to repair injuries to muscles, bones, and joints

physiology (fih-zee-AH-luh-gee) the study of the activities of the body's tissues and cells

rehabilitation (ree-uh-bi-luh-TAY-shuhn) special activities, exercises, or other programs that return an athlete to normal health after an injury

splints (SPLINTZ) pieces of wood, plastic, or metal that are used to prevent movement of a joint or to support an injured arm or leg

sprains (SPRAYNZ) stretches or tears of a ligament

strains (STRAYNZ) stretches or tears of a muscle or tendon

FOR MORE INFORMATION

Books

Careers in Focus: Physicians. New York: Ferguson Publishing, 2006.

Devantier, Alecia T., and Carol A. Turkington. *Extraordinary Jobs in Sports*. New York: Ferguson Publishing, 2007.

Sports: What Can I Do Now? (Exploring Careers for Your Future). New York: Ferguson Publishing, 2007.

Web Sites

American Medical Society for Sports Medicine: What Is a Sports Medicine Physician?
www.newamssm.org/Whatis.pdf
Print out a brochure that explains what a sports medicine physician does

Playing Games—Careers in Sports Medicine
www.diversityalliedhealth.com/features/04-05-04a.htm
Read an article about sports medicine careers

INDEX

ABOUT THE AUTHOR

Patricia K. Kummer has written more than 60 children's nonfiction books on a variety of topics. Many of her books have been about the states, other countries, natural wonders, and inventions. She also wrote Athletic Trainer in the Cool Careers series. Ms. Kummer likes researching and writing nonfiction because truth is stranger than fiction! Besides writing, she teaches adults about writing nonfiction for children, and she visits schools where she enjoys talking to children about the writing process. When she is not working, Ms. Kummer likes to read and to travel.

O 13/09